Overview Look at the Leaves

S0-FEQ-386

Leaves on deciduous trees bud, grow, and fall.

Reading Vocabulary Words

deciduous
needles
evergreen

High-Frequency Words

spring	*buds*
find	*cool*
leaves	*winter*
will	*gone*

Building Future Vocabulary

* These vocabulary words do not appear in this text. They are provided to develop related oral vocabulary that first appears in future texts.

Words:	*seasons*	*change*	*trunk*
Levels:	Library	Gold	Gold

Comprehension Strategy
Connecting ideas from text-to-world

Fluency Skill
Adjusting pace

Phonics Skill
Using knowledge of vowel dipthongs /oi/ (s<u>oi</u>l)

Reading-Writing Connection
Writing a paragraph

Home Connection
Send home one of the Flying Colors Take-Home books for children to share with their families.

Differentiated Instruction
Before reading the text, query children to discover their level of understanding of the comprehension strategy — Connecting ideas from text-to-world. As you work together, provide additional support to children who show a beginning mastery of the strategy.

Focus on ELL
- Show pictures of trees with different kinds of leaves. Discuss how seasons and weather affect the growth of leaves. Help children associate each season with the correct English term.

- Have children tell about seasons using their own drawings.

T1

Using This Teaching Version

1. Before Reading
2. During Reading
3. Revisiting the Text
4. Assessment

This Teaching Version will assist you in directing children through the process of reading.

1. **Begin with Before Reading** to familiarize children with the book's content. Select the skills and strategies that meet the needs of your children.

2. **Next, go to During Reading** to help children become familiar with the text, and then to read individually on their own.

3. **Then, go back to Revisiting the Text** and select those specific activities that meet children's needs.

4. **Finally, finish with Assessment** to confirm children are ready to move forward to the next text.

1 Before Reading

Building Background
- Write the word *deciduous* on the board. Read it aloud. Ask children to share what they know about leaves on trees. Ask *Do all trees drop their leaves?* (No, evergreens do not.) Correct any misinformation.

- Introduce the book by reading the title, talking about the cover photograph, and sharing the overview.

Building Future Vocabulary
Use Interactive Modeling Card: Word Sorter

- Introduce the word *seasons*. Write *seasons* in the top box of the Word Sorter.

- Write two different *seasons* in the next level.

- Brainstorm words to describe each *season* and write them in the Word Sorter.

Introduction to Reading Vocabulary
- On blank cards write: *deciduous*, *needles*, and *evergreen*. Read them aloud. Tell children these words will appear in the text of *Look at the Leaves*.

- Use each word in a sentence for understanding.

Introduction to Comprehension Strategy

- Explain that readers connect ideas from stories to the world around them. This helps readers to better understand the text and the world.

- Tell children to look for connections in the text to something they have experienced in life.

- Using the cover photograph and book title, have children tell when and where they have seen different-colored leaves.

Introduction to Phonics

- Write on the board: **soil**. Read the word aloud. Underline *oi*. Tell children the sound of the *o* glides into the *i*. Model the diphthong sound.

- Together read the sentences on page 8. Tell children to raise their hands when they hear a word that has a gliding vowel sound. (**soil**) Have children locate the word on the page.

- Write on the board: **oil**, **boil**, and **foil**. Read the words aloud and point out that they all have vowel sounds that glide.

Modeling Fluency

- Read aloud page 4, modeling how you adjust your reading pace for punctuation and repeated phrases.

- Point out the repeated phrases in the text. Tell children neither to rush through sentences nor to read the words as a list. Remind children to slow down for commas and pause for periods.

2 During Reading

Book Talk

Beginning on page T4, use the During Reading notes on the left-hand side to engage children in a book talk. On page 16, follow with Individual Reading.

T3

During Reading

Book Talk

- **Comprehension Strategy**
  Explain to children that when they read, they should find connections between the text and their personal experiences.

- Ask *What is this book about?* (leaves) *How do you know?* (from the title and cover photograph) *Have you ever seen red and yellow leaves?*

- Discuss the cover photograph and what children know about leaves and trees. Have children draw leaves they have seen or bring in examples.

Turn to page 2 — Book Talk

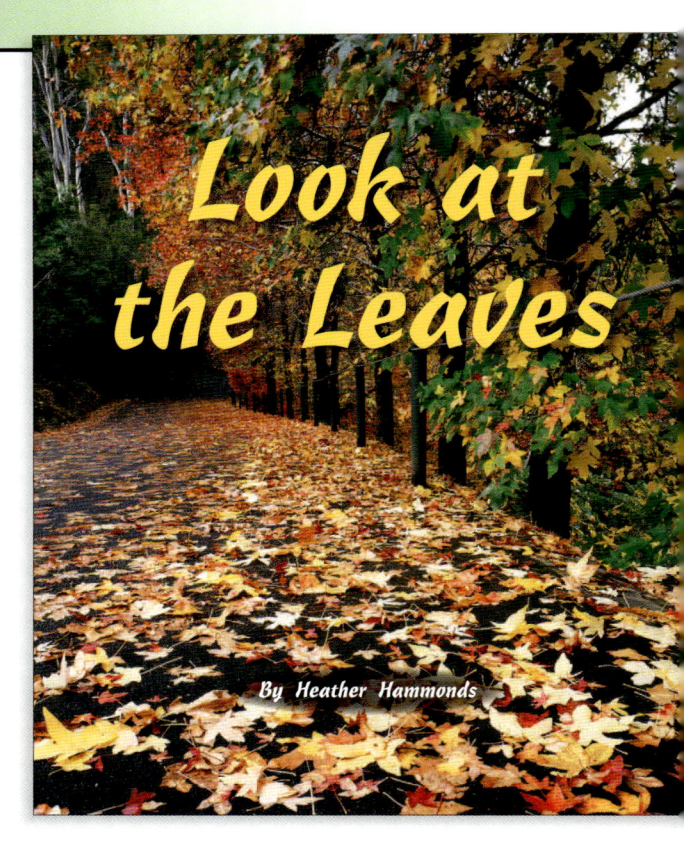

Look at the Leaves

By Heather Hammonds

Revisiting the Text

Look at the Leaves

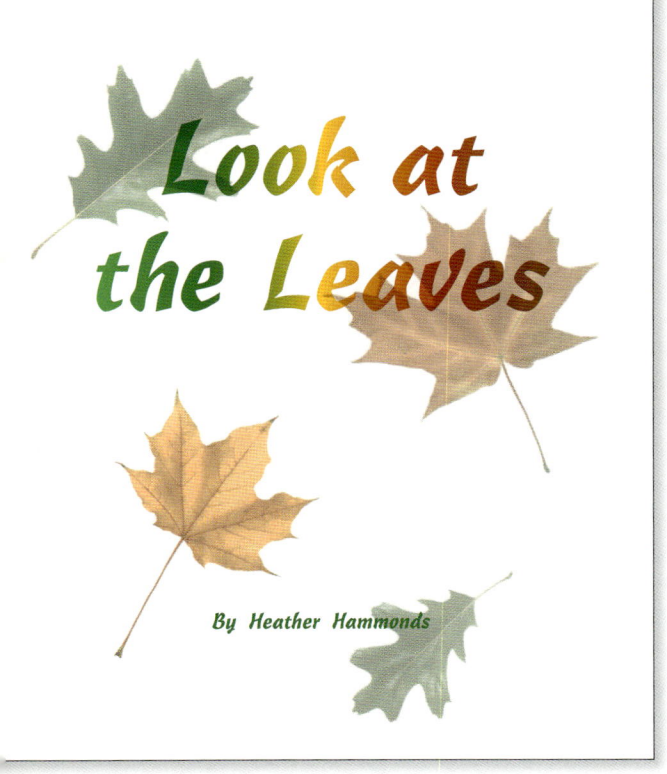

By Heather Hammonds

Future Vocabulary
- Say *Look at the cover. The leaves are different colors. What do you think causes this change?* (It is getting cold.) *What season do you think this is?* (autumn, fall)

Now revisit pages 2–3

During Reading

Book Talk
- Ask *Where do trees grow?* (in homes, forests, parks, and cities)

- **Comprehension Strategy**
  Point out the colors and shapes of leaves on pages 2 and 3. Ask *Have you ever seen tree leaves such as these? What tree names do you know?*

↪ ***Turn to page 4 — Book Talk***

Trees Around Us

We can see trees in lots of places.

There are trees on some streets.
There are trees in parks.

Revisiting the Text

There are trees in yards, and there are trees in forests.

There are trees everywhere!

Future Vocabulary
- Introduce the word *trunk*. Tell children it is the main stem of a tree. Ask *Do these trees have big trunks?* (yes) Tell children that *trunk* can also mean a large chest. Say *Some people use trunks to store clothing or other things. What kinds of things would you store in a trunk?* (toys, clothing)

Now revisit pages 4–5

During Reading

Book Talk

- Ask *What do all trees have in common?* (They all have leaves.) *Do all leaves have the same shape?* (no)

- Point to the needles on page 4. Ask *Have you seen a tree with needles? Do you know what kinds of trees have needles?* (pine trees) *Why do you think we call these leaves needles?* (because the leaves are sharp, like needles)

Turn to page 6 – Book Talk

Trees and Leaves

All trees have leaves.
Some trees have big leaves.
Some trees have little leaves.
Some trees have long,
thin leaves called needles.

Revisiting the Text

All trees need the sun.
The sun shines on their leaves.
This helps the trees to grow.

Future Vocabulary
- Show children the photograph on page 5. Ask *Do you see a tree trunk in this picture?* (no) *What parts of trees do you see?* (leaves, branches) *How are branches different from a trunk?* (They are smaller; there are more of them.)

Now revisit pages 6–7

During Reading

Book Talk

- **Comprehension Strategy** Say *Not all trees lose their leaves. We call trees that have leaves all year round evergreen trees. Have you ever seen an evergreen tree?*

- Point out that *evergreen* is made up of two smaller words, *ever* and *green.* Ask children why they think that is. (because an evergreen tree is always, or ever, green)

- Point out that the word *evergreen* is in boldfaced type. Say *Some books have features that help readers know what is important. What other word is in boldfaced type?* (deciduous) *A deciduous tree loses its leaves in the winter.* Have children discuss the question on page 7, using personal experience to support their answers.

Turn to page 8 — Book Talk

Growing Leaves

Some trees have leaves all the time.
The leaves grow in summer.
The leaves grow in winter, too.

Trees that have leaves all the time are called **evergreen** trees.

6

6

Revisiting the Text

Some trees have no leaves in winter. Trees that have no leaves in winter are called **deciduous** trees.

Will these trees grow new leaves in spring? Let's find out!

Future Vocabulary
- Explain to children that some trees change with the seasons. Ask *What kinds of trees do not change from summer to winter?* (evergreen trees) *Do you know the names of the four seasons?* (spring, summer, autumn [fall], and winter) *What season is it in the photograph on page 7?* (winter) *How can you tell?* (The trees have no leaves. There is snow on the ground.)

Now revisit pages 8–9

During Reading

Book Talk

- **Comprehension Strategy**
 Ask *Have you seen a tree budding? Have you seen trees flowering? What do they smell like? In what season do trees bud and flower?* (spring)

- **Phonics Skill** Have children locate the word *soil* on page 8. Tell them that this word blends two vowel sounds together. Ask *What two vowel sounds glide together in* soil? (the vowels *o* and *i*)

Turn to page 10 – Book Talk

In Spring

In spring, the sun shines.
It warms the soil on the ground.
The sun warms the trees, too.
Little buds on the tree branches start to grow.

buds

8

Revisiting the Text

Soon the buds open.
Some buds have flowers inside them.
Some buds have little leaves inside them.

The little leaves grow bigger and bigger.

flowers

Future Vocabulary
- Say *Look at the branches growing off the tree trunk. What is growing on the branches?* (buds) Ask *What change takes place during spring?* (The soil gets warm. Tree buds start to open.)

- **Comprehension Strategy** Ask *What else do you know about the spring season?* (It is a season of rain. Trees and plants grow. Flowers start to bloom. Bees like the flowers.)

Now revisit pages 10–11

During Reading

Book Talk
- Ask *What happens to leaves during the summer?* (They turn green.)
- **Comprehension Strategy**
  Say *Look at the people sitting under the tree. Why do people like to sit under trees during the summer?* (The leaves make shade. It is cooler under the tree.)

Turn to page 12 – Book Talk

In Summer

In summer, the flowers have gone
from the trees,
but there are lots of big,
green leaves.
The trees are growing
in the warm sun.

Revisiting the Text

It is cool under the trees.
We can sit under the trees
and have a picnic.
The leaves help us
keep out of the sun.

Future Vocabulary
- Ask *What change do leaves go through during summer?* (They start to grow. The leaves get big.) *What other changes happen during summer?* (It gets warmer. The grass turns green. It does not snow.)

Now revisit pages 12–13

During Reading

Book Talk

- Read and study pages 12–13 together. Ask *What happens to deciduous trees in autumn?* (They turn colors: yellow, red, orange, and brown.) *Do the leaves stay on the tree?* (No, they fall off.)

- **Comprehension Strategy** Say *Look at the photograph on page 13. Based on what you see, what can you tell me about the weather?* (It is cool.) *How do you know?* (The leaves are red and yellow, but some are still green.) *What happens to evergreen trees in autumn?* (The leaves do not fall off. They stay green.)

- **Fluency Skill** Have children read aloud the page, pausing for each comma and stopping at each period. Tell them to pause as though there were commas in the third sentence.

Turn to page 14 – Book Talk

In Autumn

In autumn, it is not as sunny.
Rain falls, and it is cool.
The leaves on the trees turn yellow
and red
and orange
and brown.

The wind blows, and the old leaves start to fall from the trees.
Soon there are lots of leaves on the ground.

Revisiting the Text

Future Vocabulary
- Ask *What season is it on page 13?* (It is autumn.) *How do the leaves change during this season?* (The leaves turn colors during this season. The wind blows the leaves off the trees.) *Does the trunk change during autumn?* (no)

Now revisit pages 14–15

During Reading

Book Talk
- Ask *What happens to the deciduous trees in the winter?* (The deciduous trees are bare. They do not have leaves.) *Why?* (It is cold. There is snow.) Say *You can see a tree's branches in the winter. If you look closely, what can you see on the branches?* (little buds) Ask *What will happen to the buds in spring?* (They will grow into leaves again.)

Turn to page 16 – Book Talk

In Winter

In winter, it is cold.
In some places snow falls.
All the leaves have gone
from the deciduous trees.
We can see their branches again.

Revisiting the Text

If we look at the branches of these trees in winter, we can see lots of little buds.

When spring comes, the buds will grow into leaves and flowers again.

buds

Future Vocabulary
- Say *Winter is a cold season. What happens during winter?* (It snows. The trees lose all of their leaves.) *How will the buds change when spring comes?* (They will grow into leaves.)

- **Comprehension Strategy** Encourage children to talk about seasonal changes. Say *Besides the changing leaves on trees, what other changes in nature do you notice?* (temperature, weather, flowers, birds making nests)

Go to page T5 — Revisiting the Text

15

During Reading

Book Talk
- Leave this page for children to discover on their own when they read the book individually.

Individual Reading

Have each child read the entire book at his or her own pace while remaining in the group.

Go to page T5 — Revisiting the Text

Keeping Leaves

Look at all these leaves.
We can put them inside a book and keep them!

16

During independent work time, children can read the online book at:
www.rigbyflyingcolors.com

16

3 Revisiting the Text

Future Vocabulary
- Use the notes on the right-hand pages to develop oral vocabulary that goes beyond the text. These vocabulary words first appear in future texts. These words are: *seasons*, *change*, and *trunk*.

Turn back to page 1

Reading Vocabulary Review
Activity Sheet: Word Log

- Have children write the words *deciduous*, *needles*, and *evergreen* in the Word Log.
- Ask children to find the words in the book. Tell them to read the sentences. Have them define the words based on the text.

Comprehension Strategy Review
Use Interactive Modeling Card: Making Conclusions

- Refer children to pages 2 and 3 and model making a conclusion. Ask children to provide the details.
- Have children make four more conclusions and find support in the book.

Phonics Review
- Have children say the word *soil*. Make sure they glide the vowel sounds.
- Review the words *oil*, *boil*, and *foil*. Have children write sentences with these words and take turns reading them aloud.

Fluency Review
- Partner children and have them take turns reading the sentences on pages 10–11.
- Remind children to vary their pace. Some sentences should be read more slowly. Remind children that commas are a signal to slow down.

Reading-Writing Connection
Activity Sheet: Making Conclusions

To assist children with linking reading and writing:
- Refer to page 8 and model making a conclusion based on personal experience. Have children make conclusions about trees and the seasons based on their experiences.
- Have children write a paragraph about their favorite kind of tree.

T5

4 Assessment

Assessing Future Vocabulary

Work with each child individually. Ask questions that elicit each child's understanding of the Future Vocabulary words. Note each child's responses:

- How many seasons are there? What kind of weather happens during each season?
- The leaves change with each season. How do they change?
- The trunk is the main part of a tree. What grows from the trunk that we can see?

Assessing Comprehension Strategy

Work with each child individually. Note each child's understanding of connecting ideas from text-to-world:

- What happens to a tree's leaves during the winter? Spring? Summer? Autumn?
- What kind of weather makes a tree flower?
- What kind of weather makes leaves turn colors?
- Do all trees lose their leaves?

Assessing Phonics

Work with each child individually. Write a list of words that have *oi* diphthongs. Have each child say the words and underline both vowels. Note each child's responses for understanding of *oi* diphthongs:

- Use the following words: *soil, oil, boil,* and *foil.*
- Did each child correctly glide the two vowel sounds?
- Did each child understand that words with vowel diphthongs have two distinct sounds?

Assessing Fluency

Have each child read page 12 to you. Note each child's ability to adjust his or her pace during reading:

- Was each child able to vary his or her reading speed?
- Did each child pause at commas and stop for periods?

Interactive Modeling Cards

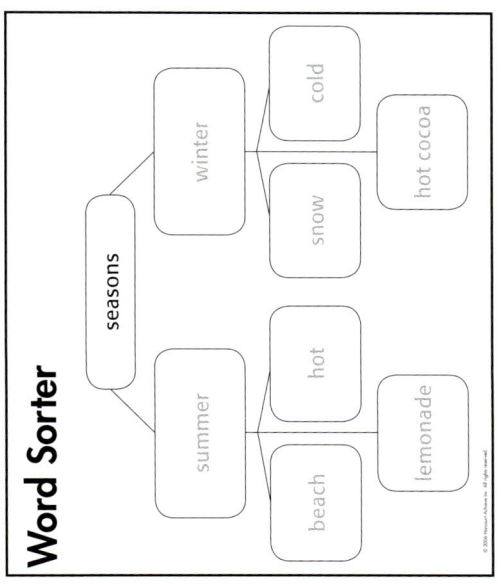

Word Sorter

seasons
- winter
  - cold
  - snow
  - hot cocoa
- summer
  - hot
  - beach
  - lemonade

Directions: With children, fill in the Word Sorter using the word *seasons*.

Making Conclusions

Conclusion	Details from the Book
Trees live in many places.	Trees are on streets, in parks, and in forests.
Leaves come in many shapes.	Some leaves are flat. Others are needle-like.
Not all trees lose their leaves.	Evergreen trees keep their leaves all year.
Some trees get new growth in spring.	As it gets warmer, trees grow buds.
Some trees' leaves are not always green.	When it gets cool, leaves can turn colors.

Directions: With children, fill in the Making Conclusions chart for *Look at the Leaves*.

Discussion Questions

- What do leaves need to make them grow? (Literal)
- What happens to deciduous trees during the spring? (Critical Thinking)
- Why do some trees lose their leaves during the winter? (Inferential)

Activity Sheets

Word Log

Title: *Look at the Leaves*

Word	Meaning from Selection
deciduous	trees that have no leaves in the winter
needles	thin, pointed leaves
evergreen	trees that have leaves all of the time

Directions: Have children fill in the Word Log using the words *deciduous*, *needles*, and *evergreen*. Have children define each word based on meanings from the text.

Making Conclusions

Conclusion	Details from the Book
Spring has arrived when trees bud.	Trees grow buds in spring.
Trees do not die when they drop their leaves.	New leaves grow back the next year.
Big trees help keep me cool during the summer.	The leaves keep out the sun.

Directions: Have children fill in the chart by making conclusions about trees and the seasons based on personal experience.

Optional: On a separate sheet of paper, have children write a paragraph about their favorite kind of tree.